Gotta Text!

REMINDERS TO LIVE OUT THE GOSPEL THROUGH EVERY DAY ENCOUNTERS

JULIA A. BROOKS

WESTBOW
P R E S S®
A DIVISION OF THOMAS NELSON
& ZONDERVAN

Scripture quotations are from the ESV® Bible (The Holy Bible, English
Standard Version®), copyright © 2001 by Crossway, a publishing ministry
of Good News Publishers. Used by permission. All rights reserved.

WestBow Press books may be ordered through
booksellers or by contacting:

WestBow Press
A Division of Thomas Nelson & Zondervan
1663 Liberty Drive
Bloomington, IN 47403
www.westbowpress.com
1 (866) 928-1240

ISBN: 978-1-9736-0107-4 (sc)
ISBN: 978-1-9736-0108-1 (e)

Library of Congress Control Number: 2017913495

Print information available on the last page.

WestBow Press rev. date: 09/05/2018

Contents

Preface.. vii

Acknowledgments ix

Introduction xi

Definition xiii

Text 1   Flawed for Now 1

Text 2   Wanted: Sin Killers 4

Text 3   Let's Get Ready to Rumble! 7

Text 4   Deeply Rooted... 10

Text 5   Hard Times 12

Text 6   Family... 14

Text 7   Debt-Free.. 16

Text 8   Gotta Represent 18

Text 9   Weather Report.. 20

Text 10 Looking Upward 23

Text 11 Adjusted Lenses... 25

Text 12 It Will Do 27

Text 13 You're Kidding Me, Right? 29

Text 14 Thorns.. 31

Text 15 Damaged Goods.. 34

Text 16 Selfies.. 36

Text 17 To the Rescue 38

Text 18 No GPS Needed 41

Text 19 A Typical Day.. 44

Text 20 The Least of These.. 46

Text 21 Stormy Weather 48

Text 22 Balloons Will Rise... 50

Text 23 Lighting the Dark... 52

Text 24 Words 54

Text 25 Body Life 57

Text 26 A Different Kind of Normal........................... 60

Text 27 Chocolate Treats (Halloween)....................... 62

Text 28 Hustle and Bustle (Christmas) 64

Text 29 The Close of the Year (New Year's Eve)......... 67

Text 30 A Song (Good Friday)..................................... 69

Text 31 Son Rise (Easter/Resurrection Day).............. 72

About the Author 77

Preface

Gotta Text! is a devotional that shares how vital the gospel message is in the rhythm of life. This book can encourage believers who, like me, need reminders to discover the gospel in their lives' journeys.

Take this thirty-one-day voyage to help you to think again of the gospel message and to see it in the simplest daily occurrences. God's message written in the English Standard Version in this devotional is not a theological exposition of the deep truths of the scriptures. It merely helps you to take stock of each day's happenings and to see the gospel message in them.

For those who do not know the gospel, my prayer is that the Holy Spirit will draw you to Him and regenerate your heart so that you can see the light of the gospel unto salvation.

Acknowledgments

IT IS WITH HUMBLE gratitude that I give thanks to Jesus Christ, who uses me as an instrument of the gospel message through the pages of this devotional. A grateful thank you goes to Marty Machowski, who mentored me in the preparation of *Gotta Text!* and without whom it might not have come to fruition. Many thanks go to Patricia Massengale for the use of her editing skills and to Doug Nottage for his technical support and insight in this project. My deepest thanks go to my best friend and husband, Julius, who believed I had a story to tell and encouraged me to put it into words.

Introduction

GOTTA TEXT! WAS CREATED to encourage those who communicate through digital devices to send uplifting messages to family and friends. The greatest text message of all times was sent to you thousands of years ago. It is God's breathed word, written in the scriptures, for revelation, instruction, and application. Thus, *Gotta Text!* becomes a vehicle to connect people with the gospel message through their daily experiences.

Gotta Text! delves into the lives of ordinary people doing ordinary things as the gospel message is revealed. These devotions are written as if a text message was sent personally to you when reading others' circumstances— the mundane and the exciting, the struggles and the victories, the daily grind and the sporadic adventures. *Gotta Text!* is an interactive devotional in which you have an opportunity to "text" a friend or a group of friends and family with a select, brief message—a reminder that God's Word is life and light that can be lived out daily. After the completion of the thirty-one-day journey, encourage your friends and family members to begin their own journeys and texting networks with *Gotta Text!*

Definition

TEXT: AN INFORMAL ABBREVIATED message communicated to inform, remind, warn or advise through digital devices.

TEXT 1
Flawed for Now

EVERYONE HAS THAT FAVORITE show to settle in and watch. One of Johnnie's favorite was National Geographic. It produced global glimpses of nature at its best. Johnnie could peek in on the migration of animals, the display of birds and sea creatures, the grandeur of the mountainsides and valleys, and the rushing waters that broke forth in shouts of the glory of God's creation.

Humankind has gone as far as to distinguish certain global sights as the Seven Wonders of the World— the Colossus of Rhodes, the Great Pyramid of Giza, the Hanging Gardens of Babylon, the Lighthouse of Alexandria, the Mausoleum at Halicarnassus, the statue of Zeus at Olympia, and the Temple of Artemis at Ephesus. Whenever Johnnie wanted to recount the beginnings of these spectacles, he turned to the book of Genesis, which narrates creation's existence by the spoken Word of God. By His Word, trees appeared and brought forth fruit, lights in the heavens separated day from night, waters swarmed with living creatures, and the earth produced livestock, creeping things, and beasts. Johnnie was also reminded how God created humankind in His image.

Creator God planted both male and female in the spectacular garden of Eden. Adam (God's prototype, representing the whole of humankind) managed the garden well—until he committed an overt act of disobedience, along with his wife, Eve, by making choices independent of the Creator. The perfect relationship was severed, and creation itself was marred. Earth, however, still had its beauty—lustrous landscapes, breathtaking waterfalls, and astonishing sunrises.

Humankind made great discoveries of treatments for diseases and humanitarian efforts to leave the world a better place. In spite of these accomplishments, there were continual wars, as nations suffered. The environment was cursed with thistles and weeds and atmospheric collisions, and animals preyed upon each other. Clearly, all was flawed but only for the present. The future paints a brighter picture. God tells us that He will one day make all things new. He reminds us that what is now flawed will one day be made perfect again.

FOR YOUR INFORMATION

Let us live in this presently flawed world, knowing that the future will bring change. We are reminded of the text in God's Word that all will be well. "Then I saw a new heaven and a new earth" (Revelation 21:1a). Therefore, let us, as believers, live in the light of God's Word with hope until He returns.

KEEP IN TOUCH—TEXT A FRIEND OR FRIENDS WITH THESE WORDS

Don't be downcast on account of past failures because Christ took care of them on the cross.

"Therefore, if anyone is in Christ, he is a new creation. The old has passed away; behold, the new has come" (2 Corinthians 5:17).

TEXT 2
Wanted: Sin Killers

SIN HAS MANY FEATURES. It pops up in our thoughts when we pray, it rises in our attitudes when someone crosses us, and it trips us up when we are ensnared by gossip and slander in the guise of a conversation. Sin requires believers to gear up for battle that lies not with man "but against the rulers, against the authorities, against the cosmic powers over this present darkness, against the spiritual forces of evil in the heavenly places" (Ephesians 6:12b). The battle of sin must be won by any means necessary because if we don't have it killed, sin will surely slay us. And if we are defeated, how, then, can we live in the light of God's Word? By the power of the Holy Spirit, we must contend.

Where there is hatred, weaken with love; where there is envy, slaughter with encouragement; with covetousness, pierce with contentment; with lies, destroy with truth; and with immorality, kill with purity of thought. This comes with some preparation.

"Let us cleanse ourselves from every defilement of body and spirit, bringing holiness to completion in the fear of God" (2 Corinthians 7:1b).

Christ will return to rule and reign on earth. He first came to rule and reign in our hearts, and through Him we can live in victory over our sins. We therefore must choose to live in righteousness for the glory of our King. As Paul reminds us, "Put on then as God's chosen ones, holy and beloved, compassionate hearts, kindness, humility, meekness and patience, bearing with one another, and if anyone has a complaint against another forgiving each other; as the Lord has forgiven you, so you must also forgive" (Colossians 3:12–13). God's power alone can kill those sins that still lie within, but you must be willing to give them over for destruction. The sin killer has already come and fought the fight on our behalf, in the person of Jesus the Christ.

FOR YOUR INFORMATION

Until Christ returns to rule and govern this world forevermore, the scriptures implore us to join in the battle of the world, the flesh, and the devil. Peter encourages us in our call to be holy in our daily pursuits by "preparing your minds for action, and being sober-minded; … As obedient children, do not be conformed to the passions of your former ignorance, but as He who called you is holy, you also be holy in all your conduct" (1 Peter 1:13a, 14–15). "For we are the temple of the living God" (2 Corinthians 6:16b).

KEEP IN TOUCH—TEXT A FRIEND OR FRIENDS WITH THESE WORDS

Don't fret over struggling with sins in your life. The world cannot hold you captive. "For everyone who has been born of God overcomes the world. And this is the victory that has overcome the world—our faith" (1 John 5:4).

TEXT 3
Let's Get Ready to Rumble!

FRIDAY EVENINGS WERE FIGHT Night on the fight channel in Ed's household. The air was full of excitement as each fighter made his grand entrance. Music blasted as he entered the ring, accompanied by his entourage. The announcer finally introduced both boxers just before the bell rang, ending with the popular phrase—joined in by both the live and television audience—"Let's get ready to ru-u-u-m-m-ble!" Unlike boxers, Christians engage in spiritual rumbles as believers in Christ. Paul's letters school us about such things. One of our battles will call for fighting the good fight of faith. Timothy's text in 2 Timothy 2:4 reminds us not to get tangled on the ropes of civilian pursuits—on the grandeur of the world. Our aim is to counter-punch that tendency and focus on pleasing the one who is Lord of our lives. Just as boxers may not always see the next punch coming, Paul warns us that we may not see the next trap set before us. Our opponent has a powerful punch which he strategically lands at the right time. The enemy attacks with blows when we least expect it. Our natural flesh can cause us to stumble in our daily walk, as easily as overreacting to a comment made to us. That is all we need to justify our ungodly response. Satan's assistants are on 24/7 alert to work on getting us to do just that. So how do we ready ourselves for those attacks? Before the warriors get into the ring, they prepare themselves. We, like the fighters, are to prepare for spiritual battle as we navigate the ring of life each day. Throughout the day, we believers have to keep our gear on to protect us from attacks that could easily send us reeling when we become impatient with others. We display bad tempers when we feel justified, show poor attitudes when we hear criticisms and corrections, and, at times, we belittle others to defend our self-esteem. Attacks will surely come, but God's armor will shield us in our responses. Paul describes in Ephesians 6:14–15 how to live among believers in the unity of faith by this spiritual preparedness. The text instructs us to "Stand therefore, having fastened on the belt of truth, and having put on the breastplate of righteousness, and as shoes for your feet, having put on the readiness given by the gospel of peace."

FOR YOUR INFORMATION

When we are dressed daily in our spiritual garb, constant in the Word, continuing in prayer and growing in grace and truth, then we too, in the spiritual realm, can be ready to rumble.

KEEP IN TOUCH—TEXT A FRIEND OR FRIENDS WITH THESE WORDS

We know the adversary. The devil prowls around to seek whom he may destroy. Remember that "the God of all grace who has called you to His eternal glory in Christ, will Himself restore, confirm, strengthen, and establish you" (1 Peter 5:10b).

TEXT 4
Deeply Rooted

It's THAT TIME OF the year when you notice gardeners in your neighborhood trimming branches and pulling weeds. A funny thing about weeds is that their roots can be quite deep. It's not so easy to pull them up sometimes. Have you ever noticed a gardener using a hand shovel to dig around the weeds in order to get down deep where the roots are? What a reminder to Christians to examine the depth of their faith.

When the season of life changes, are the roots of your faith deep enough that you can remain unmoved? True believers would not apply their faith to the soil in Matthew 13:6, when the seed fell on shallow ground. "When the sun rose up they (the seeds) were scorched. And since they had no root, they withered away." To be rooted deeply in God's Word, believers must have good soil. The Holy Spirit softens the hardness of your heart and cultivates it to be nurtured by the Word of God. The constant feeding on His Word penetrates deep in your heart, and the root system builds upon His truth. The weeds of the world's view will not be able to choke the life of the Word from you, as it is deeply planted. You become "like a tree planted by the streams of water that yields its fruit in its season, and its leaf does not wither. In all that he does, he prospers" (Psalm 1:3). Why? Because you are deeply rooted in the Word.

FOR YOUR INFORMATION

Keep your heart softened to take in the nutrients of the Word. Your response to the Word will become productive in bearing fruit. Some will produce "a hundredfold, some sixty, some thirty" (Matthew 13:8b).

KEEP IN TOUCH—TEXT A FRIEND OR FRIENDS WITH THESE WORDS

The Holy Spirit prepares your heart to grow the seeds of God's Word in you that ultimately blossom and bring forth fruit.

TEXT 5
Hard Times

"I've been homeless for only a few days," Bernie, an elderly man, said, as he began to share his story during an interview. "Whatever my situation, I am placing my trust in Jesus Christ." Bernie slept on benches, yet he found comfort in believing that God would provide for his every need. Maybe, like Bernie, it's the hard times that cause us to develop inner strength as we place our trust in the Almighty. Believers may not know how strong they are until life produces hard times to test their stability and to show them areas that they need to build up.

In 2 Corinthians 11, Paul tells of many trials he encountered. He was imprisoned multiple times; endured countless beatings, often near death; was stoned, was shipwrecked and adrift at sea; and was in constant danger during his travels. From Paul's testimony, we know he delighted in seeing his weaknesses through those times, knowing that his strength only came from the Lord. Our perfect model of handling tribulations is Christ Himself. "For the joy that was set before Him, endured the cross, despising the shame and is seated at the right hand of the throne of God" (Hebrews 12:2b). Who knows what awaits on the other side of tribulations? When shaken by life's cares, stand firm on Christ, your solid rock. As with the disciples who were once caught in a storm, Christ will be with you as He speaks peace in the midst of hard times.

FOR YOUR INFORMATION

Hard times, although they shape our character must be considered as momentary, as transient, because "this light momentary affliction is preparing for us an eternal weight of glory beyond all comparison" (2 Corinthians 4:17a).

KEEP IN TOUCH—TEXT A FRIEND OR FRIENDS WITH THESE WORDS

Don't be discouraged when hard times befall you. Lay hold of the solid rock Jesus Christ and His Word, and when the testing of your faith is over, you'll find yourself standing strong.

TEXT 6
Family

EVERY FAMILY IS DIFFERENT. Likewise, in some sports, players consider their team as a family, and their coaches are looked upon as father figures. Coaches carry a lot of responsibility. They make the calls on how long the practices will run, how many practices will be scheduled, how the plays will be executed, and who will be the game-starters. Nevertheless, the game requires commitment, hard work, and perseverance from the players. The coach is the designated figure who develops a great team. In Romans 8:15b, Paul makes the claim of a spiritual father who calls the plays in the lives of His children. They "have received the Spirit of adoption as sons, by whom we cry, 'Abba, Father!'"

Those who "receive Him, who believe in His name, He gave the right to become the children of God, who were born, not of blood, nor of the will of flesh, nor of the will of man, but of God" (John 1:12–13). God, who is your spiritual dad, makes the call on how He will orchestrate the plans for your life. His game plan is found in the scriptures, waiting for you to read and execute it through the Holy Spirit's power. One of the many orders the Father has given His children is to "love one another" (1 John 3:23b). He wants the world to see family members as objects of attention, caring for and giving tender affection to one another in such a way that the world will recognize the work of God in His spiritual family.

FOR YOUR INFORMATION

Your spiritual dad will reveal and guide you in His plans and purpose, according to His will. Although humankind is God's creation, only those who truly turn from their sins and trust in Christ will receive all the rights and privileges of being a member of His spiritual family. When asked, "Who's your daddy?" believers can always respond, "He is the Lord God Almighty."

KEEP IN TOUCH—TEXT A FRIEND OR FRIENDS WITH THESE WORDS

Remember that the scriptures are God's playbook for your life. As His children, hear His voice in the Word, and follow the plan with the help of the Holy Spirit. Each play called can be executed to perfection and for your good.

TEXT 7
Debt-Free

DRAKE WAS DOING THE old "rob from Peter to pay Paul" routine, taking money designated for one bill to pay another. Some of us, like Drake, can certainly relate to the daily challenge of paying off debt. Mortgages, student loans, car notes, or consolidated loans hopefully will not last our lifetimes. A few of us will gladly get up in the morning, grateful that we have employment as a means to pay down debt. Others grudgingly roll out of bed, dreading the trip to work but enduring it as a necessary misfortune to satisfy their debtors. Both look forward to the day—hopefully—when they can live debt-free. That's good news.

What is not so good news is the insurmountable IOU you can never pay off to God. When you sin against an infinite God, your infinite debt to Him can never be satisfied. A lifetime of good works will never balance the scales as long as the record of the infinite sin debt is held against you.

Once a people without hope of ever settling their score with the Almighty God and Judge, God, in His love for us, settled it Himself. He took the greatest debt we will ever owe and wrote "paid in full" on our accounts with His Son's blood. According to Colossians 2:13b–14, "...having forgiven us all our trespasses, by canceling the record of debt that stood against us with its legal demands. This He set aside, nailing it to the cross." We live spiritually debt-free in light of the gospel. Paying down monthly debt takes on a new perspective when you know that your spiritual debt is paid in full.

FOR YOUR INFORMATION

There are many finance agencies to help you get control of your debt and ultimately become debt-free. Jesus the Christ, however, is your only option when it comes to being debt-free for the payment for your sins. It's the only way to bypass God's wrath that is to come, and it's yours for the taking through faith in Him who made it possible.

KEEP IN TOUCH—TEXT A FRIEND OR FRIENDS WITH THESE WORDS

You may be in debt from obtaining worldly accruals, but remember that Jesus paid the eternal debt of your sin to the Father.

TEXT 8
Gotta Represent

SOME HOMETOWN SPORTS LOYALISTS are really devoted to ensuring that no out-of-town fans seated in their midst feel welcome or (in some instances) safe. Visitors enter the hometown's territory and sit among their rivals at their own possible peril. Geared up in their team's sportswear, both opposing sides are ready and determined to demonstrate team spirit by wearing team numbers on T-shirts, painting team colors on their faces, and putting on oversized hats and other team symbols for show.

In like manner, believers are called to represent as members of God's team, especially when they rival other gods. Although Christ embraced those who lived and thought differently than He did (and ate at their tables), He did not condone their behaviors. Christ encountered much ridicule among some who despised His teachings. Where then does that leave you, engaging in a community of diverse beliefs, some of which may not accept Christ, whom you represent? Understand that ridicule is likely when you live publicly the gospel truths you declare in your heart. Matthew's writings (Matthew 5:11–12) spell out the possibility of being reviled, persecuted and falsely accused for Christ's sake.

Your mandate is to rejoice in those circumstances of persecution, knowing the promise that your reward will be great. You may not receive it here on earth but will in the life to come, which is eternal. So clothe yourself in the truth of His Word and represent!

FOR YOUR INFORMATION

You are living in times where believers are stigmatized as intolerant because they hold true to the scriptures. Attacks may become more frequent because of your steadfastness to publicly live out your faith. Paul gives encouragement to fight the good fight. What sufferings you may experience on earth's journey cannot be compared to "what God has prepared for those who love Him" (1 Corinthians 2:9).

KEEP IN TOUCH—TEXT A FRIEND OR FRIENDS WITH THESE WORDS

In your determination to become more Christ-like in the power of the Holy Spirit, endeavor to stand strong when assailed for your biblical beliefs. And in so standing, you truly will represent Him, who represented you while on the cross.

TEXT 9
Weather Report

"EXPECT A HEAVY FOG this morning," started the typical weather forecast from London's iPad. "Drivers, please make sure your headlights are on, and pedestrians, look out for cars that may not come to a complete stop at the crossing."

So much for clear skies and a cool day, London thought as she grabbed her coffee on her way out the door. A second later, the door swung open again, just wide enough for London to retrieve the bright yellow umbrella in the stand. Finally off to work, she took the flight of stairs down to the garage, where her sedan was parked close to the exit. She buckled-in while starting the car, and then London switched on the radio, took a sip of her freshly brewed mocha latte, shifted the gear to drive, and quickly made her way into the bumper-to-bumper traffic. The fog was thick as forecasted, which caused London to swerve just a bit when she almost hit the jeep in front of her. *How am I going to drive the next twenty minutes in this mess?*, the voice in her head asked when she spotted the rear lights of the cars passing her. London realized that if she kept a close distance behind the car ahead of her, she could safely drive by following that car's rear lights.

Fog in the spiritual sense is just as blinding. Like London, we are looking for a light to follow in those moments of uncertainty. Who is to say whether God is creating these fogs for a specific purpose? Living in a fog for a season may be part of the preparation "to equip us for every good work" (2 Timothy 3:17b). A spiritual fog can position us toward total dependency on Christ, as He is building up our faith and character. When we're in a spiritual fog, the scriptures become our headlights and our pathway. The next time you hear the weather report warning you of fog heading your way, keep in mind that God sends His own spiritual fog without a warning. When you see such a fog forming, know that something special is about to happen. Stay the course, even though you cannot see the steps ahead. Your comfort comes from knowing that God alone is your guiding Light. He will lead you through His Word.

FOR YOUR INFORMATION

When in a spiritual fog, turn to the scriptures. The Word will sharpen your spiritual eyesight to better discern the path you are on. When you can't see your way or know where your turning point comes, "your ears shall hear a Word behind you saying, 'This is the way, walk in it'" (Isaiah 30:21a).

KEEP IN TOUCH—TEXT A FRIEND OR FRIENDS WITH THESE WORDS

When the Father sends a spiritual fog in your life, receive it as an opportunity to be guided by the light of His Word.

TEXT 10
Looking Upward

"FIFTEEN MINUTES LEFT, CLASS," the teacher announced. Connie looked at her paper to count how many problems remained. She could see in her peripheral vision that Monty was gazing at the ceiling. Connie briefly glanced in his direction, hoping to get his attention to indicate he should get back to work, but it was to no avail. Monty continued to stare as if he were in another time and place.

"Okay, everyone, time's up. Turn in your papers, read the next three chapters, and we will meet next week," came the final instruction from the teacher.

"How did you do?' Connie asked as she and Monty walked down the hall. "Just fine," he responded. Monty went on to explain how he applied a concept, learned in a previous session, that helped him take that test and finish early.

"I look up, and I can visualize the problems, which helps me to solve them faster," he explained.

That concept is nothing new. Hundreds of years ago, Paul encouraged believers to "seek the things that are above, where Christ is, seated at the right hand of God. Set your minds on the things that are above, not on things that are on the earth" (Colossians 3:1b, 2). It is logical for believers to be guided to seek what lies in the heavenly realm, where Christ is.

The biblical view implies if we engage Christ, who is seated on the throne above, then we likely will be more focused on how He governs and guides us on earth, and we likely will live out the heavenly values in this world. "Your kingdom come, your will be done, on earth as it is in heaven" (Matthew 6:10).

FOR YOUR INFORMATION

There's no need to be overly concerned about how this world views life. However, as we approach earthly responsibilities, we ought to "seek first the kingdom of God and His righteousness" (Matthew 6:33a). This should influence our perspective within the society we engage.

KEEP IN TOUCH—TEXT A FRIEND OR FRIENDS WITH THESE WORDS

"Looking to Jesus, the founder and perfecter of our faith" (Hebrews 12:2a), will help us to see life from a biblical perspective as we set our minds on things above.

TEXT 11
Adjusted Lenses

IT'S THAT TIME OF the year when scheduling an eye examination is placed on your list of things to do. On Saturday morning you find yourself placing your left hand over your left eye to read the letters from the top down. Matthew draws our attention to a spiritual eye examination when he speaks of the Christian's range of vision with the question, "Why do you see the speck that is in your brother's eye, but do not notice the log that is in your own eye?"(Matthew 7:3). Spiritual blinders can make nearsighted believers quick to spot close-up character flaws or make farsighted believers see faulty behavior in others from a distance, but they don't see their own shortcomings. Physical eyesight can be adjusted with the help of prescription lenses, but only by the work of the Holy Spirit are we able to spiritually see and understand the mind of Christ.

Believers' spiritual birth comes with spiritual insight also. Christians adjust their spiritual vision through the Word of God and see the world through their Father's eyes. May God give all believers spiritual 20/20 vision to do just that.

FOR YOUR INFORMATION

"Whoever does what is true, comes to the light, so that it may be clearly seen that his works have been carried out in God" (John 3:21).

KEEP IN TOUCH—TEXT A FRIEND OR FRIENDS WITH THESE WORDS

When you realize that you are engrossed in the world's perspective in response to your life, allow the Holy Spirit to adjust your lens through God's Word.

TEXT 12
It Will Do

CHARLENE WAS GETTING THE ingredients together for the lasagna when three-year-old Sherry wanted to be Mom's helper. Charlene opened a special cabinet designated just for Sherry; it was close to the counter and contained lots of neatly placed but mismatched bowls and tops. "You can help me bake some cookies, Sherry. Can you hand me one of your mixing bowls so we can start?"

Sherry looked around her special cabinet and pulled out a small square pan. "How is this one?" she asked. Her mom replied, "It will do." It wasn't the right size or shape, but Charlene had a knack for taking misshaped items and making them useful.

We have witnessed how God uses our small offerings for His purposes. God displays Himself in our circumstances, not by relying on our resources being sufficient but by taking the little we have and saying, in a sense, "It will do." Jesus's feeding five thousand men in addition to women and children with a poor boy's meager lunch of five barley loaves and two fish is one of many examples.

With a rod, God used Moses to demonstrate His power to part the Red Sea for Israel to cross over to their Promised Land. With a trumpet blast and a shout from Israel's soldiers, Jericho's wall fell down after a seven-go-round march. With three hundred men, Gideon subdued the Midianites. With the jawbone of a donkey, Samson slew a thousand men, and with a sling and five smooth stones, David struck down the giant, Goliath.

Our ultimate success comes when we place our resources in the Master's hand. Thus, hopes and desires can be used either to pilot our paths, which may give us a few meager accolades, or to place our limited resources in the hands of the Provider and see how He makes much of our little for His good pleasure.

FOR YOUR INFORMATION

You need not concern yourselves with how God will use your small resources. However meager your capital, our Father will take it and make it useful. "It will do," He will always tell you. "It will do."

KEEP IN TOUCH—TEXT A FRIEND OR FRIENDS WITH THESE WORDS

When you find yourself with limited resources, trust in the One who owns the world and all that is in it. He will provide.

TEXT 13
You're Kidding Me, Right?

THE HOCKEY TEAM HAD been celebrating their championship win for a week when Ryan's mom informed him that he would be playing in a different sport next year. "Something less physically challenging," she concluded because of the injuries he had sustained that year.

"You're kidding me, right?" was Ryan's response.

There may have been a time when God made such a claim on our lives, and we too echoed the same phrase— "You're kidding me, right?" Our heavenly Father has a way of dropping a bomb on our dreams and hopes while guiding us to a change of plans we normally might not embrace, and we may find ourselves asking the same question. Proverbs 16:9 tells us, "The heart of a man plans his way, but the Lord establishes his steps."

Perhaps God's directions are not your preferences. Let's take a moment and remember that your life is not your own. You gave it to Christ when He redeemed you on the cross. Fear may come when you think that God may call you to do something out of your comfort zone or even something you do not desire.

Does God give us the desires of our hearts? Of course He does, when we "seek first the kingdom of God and His righteousness" (Matthew 6:33). When God's good pleasure becomes your daily prayer, you will find yourself embracing the very desires He has for you, and when He disrupts your plans for His, you will be ready for the move. No kidding.

FOR YOUR INFORMATION

"The heart of man plans his way, but the Lord establishes his steps" (Proverbs 16:9). Although you make plans for your life, be open when detours come your way. The Lord just might want to guide you in a better direction.

KEEP IN TOUCH—TEXT A FRIEND OR FRIENDS WITH THESE WORDS

Do not despair when you sense God's calling you toward something new and different. Whatever He calls you to do, He will be faithful to make you competent and equipped to complete the task.

TEXT 14
Thorns

BECKY HAD TO MAKE a dash to the flower shop on her way to her friend's concert. The bell over the flower shop door rang as she stepped inside, informing the shopkeeper that a customer was entering.

"Can I help you?" a voice sang out from the back. The florist walked out to the front of the shop and over to the counter.

"Yes, please, I would like a bouquet for a special friend who is performing in a concert tonight."

"Any special colors you would like included?" the florist asked.

"She likes pink and purple and green," Becky answered.

The florist returned to the back of the shop to design a decorative bouquet of flowers. A moment later, Becky heard the creak in the worn wooden floor, giving notice that the florist is returning. "Careful when you put them in water," the florist cautioned her as she stepped around the counter. "The roses have a few thorns." Thorns and getting pricked come not only from beautiful roses but also from humankind, when sin shows its colors. Like the beautiful roses Becky purchased, believers have a few thorns that may prick those around them. Circumstances can strip you of good intensions and reveal thorns of discontentment, despondency, or despair. There is no getting around thistles and thorns that so easily tear and cut into your character, and as a result injures others.

Most dreadful of all were the thorns of our sins that Christ endured on the cross. He wore a crown of thorns upon his head, but He endured the sin of thorns on the cross to satisfy God's wrath on humankind. Happily, the believers' sin-filled thorns have been swallowed up in victory. Pruning remains to be done, as the Holy Spirit begins to mold us into Christ-likeness.

There may be moments when a thorn or two will shoot out through our character because the old thorny man still resides within us, but the Holy Spirit will remind us of our thorns so we can quickly confess them to the Lord. Those who walk in our paths may be spared being pricked by our thorns when we take time to commune with Christ and abide in Him. Christ is sufficient to produce in us His spiritual fruit of "love, joy, peace, patience, and kindness" (Galatians 5:22a) that stems from His vine, where we are attached.

FOR YOUR INFORMATION

When you have one of those days when hurtful actions seem to jump out of you, remember that God's grace is sufficient to overcome those actions through Christ, in whom you can do all things.

Keep in Touch—Text a Friend or Friends with These Words

Don't be discouraged if you slip up today with an ungracious action. Each time you confess it to Christ, He will give you a spiritual washing and the grace to overcome it.

TEXT 15
Damaged Goods

THE PACKAGE WAS LEFT by the side of the screen door, just where Reece requested. He grabbed the package and then found a pair of scissors in the drawer of a small table in the foyer to cut through the layers of tape. Finally, he lifted the top flap of the box and unwrapped his long-awaited gift. Reece's eyes beheld the art work that had taken him six months to find, but to his dismay, it was cracked and chipped. What he held was not the exceptional art piece he had so admired but damaged goods. Reece purchased the piece with the understanding that it was nonreturnable. It did not appear that the art work could be repaired, so it was not worth keeping.

Man was once packaged as a pristine image of God. At a moment in time, God's creation became damaged goods. When God held back the flap of the heavens and looked down into His treasured garden, He knew that sin had corrupted the once-perfect image of Him in man. God was not surprised. He was aware before He created the world that humankind would be marred by disobedience, chipped by lies, torn by pride, cracked from immorality, and ripped by anger. Nonetheless, God chose not to throw humankind away. Instead, like a potter who refashions his damaged goods, He refashioned man through His Son Jesus Christ. God didn't destroy the old self but placed a new self in those who believe in His Son.

The scriptures lovingly inform us in 2 Corinthians 5:17 that we are new creatures in Christ. Therefore, the old nature is defeated, and the new is championed. Damaged goods are remade by the Holy Spirit as special goods for the use of our King in His kingdom. He doesn't repair; He remakes.

FOR YOUR INFORMATION

God will make all things new, as written in Revelations 21:1, with a new heaven and earth. He already made you new in Christ when you placed your faith in Him.

KEEP IN TOUCH—TEXT A FRIEND OR FRIENDS WITH THESE WORDS

You can have hope in the future. Your present state of damaged goods ultimately will be made new, with a glorious body to behold the Christ who gave His life for you.

TEXT 16
Selfies

Everyone was on the bus except Arleen. She had to take two more selfies with the executive chef at the restaurant. Arleen watched his cooking show every week, and running into him today was an opportunity that she was not going to miss. "No one will believe I saw Cal if I don't take pictures to prove it," she yelled at the bus driver, who was trying to get her on the bus. "Just a second," she assured him. "One more minute, and I'll be done."

Two snapshots later, Arleen was jumping on the bus, beside herself with excitement. "Sorry about the extra time, but I was not leaving without my pictures with Cal," she said after reading the driver's expression. Arleen sat down, justifying that holding up the bus was worth it.

Perhaps there are selfies you take and share; perhaps you can relate to Arlene's obsession with capturing her likeness in the presence of a "star". No selfie, however, can capture the picture of God's justice pouring out His punishment, which we deserved, to Christ on the cross. Moreover, no selfie can reflect God's mercy for us by having Jesus pay the price to satisfy the stench of our offenses to the Father.

When you plan to take the next selfie, keep in mind the imagined selfie with Jesus on public display redeeming us from eternal destruction. When we linger on this selfie, it is possible that the effect of His selfless act may cause us to demonstrate to friends and family new selfies of Christ living through us in our daily walk.

FOR YOUR INFORMATION

"Let each of you look not only to his own interests, but also to the interests of others" (Philippians 2:4). This principle was modelled by our Lord. Remember that Christ selflessly remained faithful to the Father's mission to intercede on our behalf at Calvary. He did this instead of pursuing a less painful way, i.e. "…let this cup pass." Instead he uttered, "nevertheless, not as I will, but as You will" (Matthew 26:39).

KEEP IN TOUCH—TEXT A FRIEND OR FRIENDS WITH THESE WORDS

When you look at your selfie shots, remember Christ's imagined selfie, having selflessly died on the cross for your sins, so that you can experience peace with God.

TEXT 17
To the Rescue

It was a scorching day in August, and the Castey family could not wait to dive into the pool at the lodge where they were spending their vacation. They had just finished checking in and barely made it in their rooms before suitcases were flung open, clothes were thrown in drawers, and food was placed in the kitchen cabinets.

"Let's check out the pool," one of the kids said, and everyone headed out the door. Down the winding staircase they walked while taking in the sights. They followed the smell of chlorine to the pool, where they found the staff rearranging furniture and adding extra lighting to the area. A sign tacked on the wall by the entrance doors informed all that there would be no lifeguard on duty that day. Dad suggested that they go to the game room instead.

"We can still get in the pool," one of the kids insisted. "It's just at our own risk, like the sign says."

"I don't want to take that risk," Dad replied. "If an accident happens while you're in the pool, I can't help you.

The lifeguard is the designated person to come to your rescue, and no one is on duty."

Dad was more comfortable with the thought of a lifeguard watching everyone enjoy their swim. A lifeguard would know how to recognize signs of distress and would be the first to respond and rescue.

Although we cannot see them, many potential accidents have been interrupted by what some believe are guardian angels who protect men, women, and children from harm. They are considered our spiritual lifeguards. For thousands of years, an enormous rescue mission has been on the move. Paul's text in Colossians 1:13–14 tells of such an act. "He has delivered us from the domain of darkness and transferred us to the kingdom of His beloved Son, in whom we have redemption, the forgiveness of sins."

The ultimate Lifeguard came to earth through a virgin birth. He has already made the greatest rescue of all. Jesus Christ delivered believers from the penalty of sin. Although the wages of sin is death, those in the safety net of Christ have been rescued from the wrath that sin brings and the spiritual death that follows and are given a safe haven in Christ, with eternal life to enjoy.

FOR YOUR INFORMATION

Here lies the mandate. We who have been redeemed must rescue the perishing with vigor, as in a race. Those who live under the wrath of God must be told that there is a way to be rescued, and that is through Jesus Christ our Lord.

KEEP IN TOUCH—TEXT A FRIEND OR FRIENDS WITH THESE WORDS

Do you feel like you're drowning today with no safety net to pull you in? Jesus is quick to come to your rescue in that area of need. Take His lifeline. He has already carried your sins at the cross, so let Him carry you now.

TEXT 18
No GPS Needed

"Having a GPS is great," Mike said to himself. "Granted, they're not perfect, but they get you there." And with that, Mike spoke the location into the microphone, and off he went.

"Make a left at the corner in five hundred feet," the voice of the GPS told him.

"Perfect! Great timing!" he shouted, feeling smug about the convenience of a GPS. There was, however, another destination he would later discover without the aid of such a device. If Mike had made an attempt to get directions for this place, his Global Positioning System would have responded, "Destination unknown."

There is no address to reference the road that Mike would soon discover. This road is revealed to those who are saved by grace through faith in Christ Jesus. They will be guided to this destination by the breathing Word of God Himself. God will lead Mike, as He has led countless others, to the road called "Holiness."

If you were to pass by, you would not find skyscrapers

or malls or restaurants or hotels on this road. Instead, you would observe the activities of those journeying on this course. You would see how believers who travel there care for the mistreated, the misguided, and the unfortunate. On this road you would find people of the faith, living lives obedient to the Word of God from which they study. The Word not only guides their lives but also equips them to participate in every good work. They live out what the scriptures require—speaking truth to their neighbors and doing honest work with their hands. No corrupt talk is heard from their mouths; they use their conversations to build up each other (Ephesians 4:25–29).

If you were to come close enough, you would hear conversations among those believers that consisted of gentle and encouraging words to one another, while humbly looking out for the welfare of all. You would notice how they carry each other's burdens while singing songs of worship to their God.

Those who seek to find this road first must be "delivered from the domain of darkness and be transferred to the kingdom of God's Beloved Son" (Colossians 1:13). God Himself places you in his spiritual family, for no GPS can take you there.

FOR YOUR INFORMATION

"And a highway shall be there, and it shall be called the Way of Holiness." (Isaiah 35:8a)

KEEP IN TOUCH—TEXT A FRIEND OR FRIENDS WITH THESE WORDS

We are always going places, trying to find our way. There is a road that leads to living the holy way of life that God has chosen for us. Jesus Christ is our guide. Trust His Word, and follow Him.

TEXT 19
A Typical Day

THE DOOR OPENED, AND the nurse peered out and called Sharla's name, indicating Sharla should follow her to an examination room. She pointed to the dressing area, where Sharla was to exchange her stylish two-piece pants outfit for a bold-print hospital gown. Twenty minutes later, she found herself in a cozy lounge, glancing at the pictures in a magazine, while waiting for the nurse to peep around the corner and tell her that everything is fine and to get dressed.

Only it didn't happen that way. Thirty minutes later, Sharla was still waiting for that friendly voice. Her heart began pounding, and her breathing was shallow. *I just had an examination last year, and I was fine*—this was her consoling thought. The technician opened the door and led Sharla once again to the exam room.

"I need to take another picture for the doctors to read. It's probably nothing," the technician said.

Sharla's experience of what seemed to be a typical day was not so typical. Crises don't give warnings when making their arrival, leaving you stunned, blind-sided,

44

and off balanced. Trials are custom-designed just for you. God knows which buttons to push to get your attention and focus on Him. As with a father whose child runs to him after a bad fall, your heavenly Father is looking to catch you in His arms. When you can't feel His presence in the midst of your crisis, what do you do?

In times like Sharla experienced, when life throws you a gut punch, recall the seemingly same punch Jesus probably received in the garden of Gethsemane as He was praying, waiting to be delivered into the hands of his enemies. He knows and cares about your despair, for He is the Lord, your God, who has gone before you and already has experienced your sorrow.

FOR YOUR INFORMATION

"Fear not for I am with you, be not dismayed, for I am your God; I will strengthen you, I will help you, I will uphold you with my righteous right hand" (Isaiah 41:10).

KEEP IN TOUCH—TEXT A FRIEND OR FRIENDS WITH THESE WORDS

Nothing takes God unaware. Take hold of Him in trying times.

TEXT 20
The Least of These

HAVE YOU EVER BEEN caught at a red light and spotted someone walking between the lanes, tapping on the windows of each car while holding a sign and a rusty cup? You see the person headed in your direction. He shuffles his feet and is dressed in layers of clothing, even in the eighty-degree weather. He is persistent in asking each driver for change. Your eyes are fixed on the cup in his hand, well aware that the homeless man will soon be at your car window and ask the same question he probably has repeated a hundred times already that morning. You have to make a quick decision. Will you roll down your window and give this less fortunate person whatever change you have? Here he comes, almost to you—and then the light turns green.

There was another opportunity to help the less fortunate when you pulled the flyer from your mailbox that advertised the "Food Drive" project for the food bank. You just have to drop off the bag of groceries at your local post office, which is down the street from you.

Is it worth the effort for you to pull out a brown paper bag from the garage and check your cabinets for dry goods to share?

Attending to the "least of these" is the Christ-like response to the homeless and others as you encounter them in your daily pursuits. An encouraging word, a smile, a greeting, or taking the time to empty your pockets of change for the needy are opportunities to serve God in the most unsuspecting ways. (Matthew 25:34–40).

FOR YOUR INFORMATION

Christ identifies with us. We are paying homage to Him when we visit the sick, the imprisoned, or the downtrodden, in our families and our communities.

KEEP IN TOUCH—TEXT A FRIEND OR FRIENDS WITH THESE WORDS

You don't have to go far to serve God. Look to your left and to your right and start where you see the need. God is there, waiting for you to care for the "least of these."

TEXT 21
Stormy Weather

KATE JUST HEARD THE breaking weather report. She went to her phone and began a series of calls, first to her Aunt Emmie and then to several family members. After a few failed attempts to make contact, Kate called her niece, Carla, trying to locate Emmie, who lived alone.

"Oh yes, I picked her up yesterday, so she will be with us for the next few days until the storm subsides. We are prepared for it," Carla assured Kate. Relieved that Aunt Emmie was secure with Carla, Kate continued with her to-do list which included listening to continual weather updates.

We look to the meteorologist who reports and forecasts the atmospheric conditions with respect to clear skies, misty mornings, humid afternoons, cool evenings, and possible scattered showers. Similarly, precipitation occurs in unpredictable ways not only in the atmosphere but displays itself through our lives in the sudden loss of employment, or with unexpected and heartbreaking news. No matter if the whirlwinds of chaos flow, or the tempest of dissension rise, take shelter in the ultimate Weatherman. He not only regulates the weather but provides the shelter when the storm comes. Jesus spoke peace to the winds and the waves in the midst of a storm with His disciples. He speaks peace to the winds and the waves of our anxieties, our fears, and our despondency. Christ has already weathered the storm on the cross. He will be the captain that will guide you through the dark seas of life when you can't find your way. Let Him govern your path.

FOR YOUR INFORMATION

"Fear not, for I have redeemed you; I have called you by name, you are mine. When you pass through the waters, I will be with you" (Isaiah 43: 1b-2a).

KEEP IN TOUCH—TEXT A FRIEND OR FRIENDS WITH THESE WORDS

When the storms of life overwhelm you, remember that the ultimate Weatherman, who speaks peace to your circumstances, also can cause the winds and the waves of your adversity to cease.

TEXT 22
Balloons Will Rise

THERE IS NOTHING AS disappointing as purchasing a bouquet of balloons, and just as you are placing them in the car, somehow the ribbons unfold from around your wrist, and all you can do is watch them soar up and away. Josie wanted to make sure that didn't happen to her when she entered the store to place her order. Her eyes were racing back and forth, trying to spot the perfect balloon samples from those pinned to the wall. Finally, she picked a half dozen balloons and asked the cashier to blow them up and then tie the ribbons together with the decorative balloon weight she handed her.

Paul reminds us, as he did the believers at Ephesus, to "be filled with all the fullness of God" (Ephesians 3:19b), so as not to be weighed down with self-centeredness as if to infer that if saints are not filled with God's fullness, our tendency is to stray from Him. To be God-filled, we have to "lay aside every weight and sin which clings so closely" (Hebrews 12:1b). The weight of this world that so easily entangles us has been cut loose since we are in

Christ. Like balloons that rise when no weights are tied to them, we who are filled with the Holy Spirit can rise to good works and be fruitful to the glory of God, because sin does not weigh us down.

FOR YOUR INFORMATION

Remember that Christ has already taken the weight of our sins upon Himself, we too can soar like eagles when we confess our sins to Him who will cleanse us from all unrighteousness.

KEEP IN TOUCH—TEXT A FRIEND OR FRIENDS WITH THESE WORDS

If you are feeling weighed down with the cares of the world, or burden of sin, lighten your load onto Jesus, for He bids you to come.

TEXT 23
Lighting the Dark

It was dusk, and the boys began gathering empty jars for the capture. "As soon as you see one light up, let me know," called out a youngster from the porch swing.

"Sure thing," responded the starry-eyed ten-year-old who was standing near the curb in anticipation of twilight. With jars in their hands and eyes scanning the evening sky, Josh and Jacob patiently waited for the light show. "Here's one," Josh said and bolted in an attempt to grasp the flash of light in the palm of his hand. "Another flash should show up soon," was his encouraging remark to Jacob.

In the next moment, the boys were surrounded by flashes. Josh and Jacob began running and jumping and bumping into each other, trying to catch the lightning bugs.

"I got one!"

"I got two!"

The boys continued trying to catch as many lightning bugs as possible. It was easy to spot the flashes of light in the night—and it was worth the wait they had endured.

Only when darkness descends does the light show

begin. Maybe that's the message God is giving to those who walk in darkness. Perhaps the world is waiting for a light show, one that will illuminate hope in the depths of their souls. Maybe the called-out ones are to call those in despair into the light. The darkness in the darkest of rooms will scatter when light appears. How much more will darkness scatter in the souls of men when the light of the gospel shines before them?

Believers have the potential to create the greatest light show on earth when each one unites in the light of the gospel message and lights the souls of men.

FOR YOUR INFORMATION

"I am the Light of the world," Jesus reminds us, "Whoever follows Me will not walk in darkness, but will have the light of life" (John 8:12b).

KEEP IN TOUCH—TEXT A FRIEND OR FRIENDS WITH THESE WORDS

If you are into being a light-reflector, shine the light of the gospel on others today. They just might be in a dark place that could use the light of the Word to guide their paths.

TEXT 24
Words

"I CAN'T BELIEVE YOU said that!" Desiree exclaimed.
"No, that's not what I meant," Joanie interrupted. "I didn't mean it that way."

And so goes the conversation between two best friends. Words. What can we say about them? We stumble over words, we are tripped up by words, and we misinterpret words. Words can save us or condemn us by the testimony of others. "With it we bless our Lord and Father and with it we curse people who were made in the likeness of God," (James 3:9) according to the apostle James. "No human being can tame the tongue. It is a restless evil, full of deadly poison." (James 3:8).

We end our conversations on the phone with pleasantries and in the next second, we yell at the kids because they're late coming down for breakfast. We smile and say, "Good morning," to our neighbor and then curse the driver who cuts the corner a little too close.

We are pleasant in line at the supermarket—until someone cuts in front of us, and we inform that person, with an attitude and a few choice words, that the line is in the back.

In summary, there are moments when we speak words of comfort, kindness, and encouragement. Conversely, there are more times than we may admit when we use words to gossip or deceive or to infer a meaning by the lack of words we use. It's natural. It's what we do. Yet there is a host of those who desire to live for Him who died for them and are frustrated at times when they speak words that do not edify. Their hearts' desires are to send forth their words on a bed of soft tones that turn away wrath. Those of faith in Christ recognize the power of God's words to heal and to save. Believers understand that His words give clarity to the confused, give strength to the weak, and raise up those in despair.

Most importantly, Christians make use of God's words to give the gospel to those who are in need of a Savior. May we use God's words today to nurture the needy, to soothe the downhearted, and to calm the fears in those whose paths we cross.

FOR YOUR INFORMATION

"My son, be attentive to my words; incline your ear to my sayings. Let them not escape from your sight; keep them within your heart. For they are life to those who find them, and healing to all their flesh." (Proverbs 4:20–22).

KEEP IN TOUCH—TEXT A FRIEND OR FRIENDS WITH THESE WORDS

The Word, which is Christ Himself, became flesh for our sake. Let us use His words to heal, to comfort, and to point others to Christ for eternal life.

TEXT 25
Body Life

IT WAS ONE OF those "I can't believe this just happened" moments. On the first passing of the baton, Carie dropped it, thinking she had passed it to her teammate. Her teammates thought they were going to lose for sure. They recognized that the competition was close, and their fiercest competitors were on their heels. The seconds that followed showed how teamwork was displayed at its best. They trained independently for months before the competition to build their skills, and they worked together as one unit toward the goal of finishing first. Each member realized the position she was given, whether the starter, who created a lead, or in the middle position, who maintained the lead, or the last position, the anchor, whose job was to make up any deficits if, as in this case, the baton dropped.

What occurred next was as if the girls were swept up with miracle dust. The next teammate increased her speed as did the following two relay team members. They took a slight lead and kept it just long enough to finish strong, leaving friends and family doing a victory dance. Their competitive training had paid off.

Correspondingly, we can see the pay off in a spiritual training. It is designed for both individual gain and for building up and strengthening the body of believers in Christ, who is our head. Paul reminds us in Ephesians 4 that we were given gifts "to equip the saints in the work of ministry, for the building up of the body of Christ" (Ephesians 4:12a).

When life's demands cause us to drop the baton, it is the body of Christ, the spiritual family of believers, who have been building up each other, who can take the baton and run alongside us. Believers who engage with each other through encouragement, through prayer, and by using their gifts to help one another, demonstrate the out working of body-life among the saints in ordinary circumstances. Christian body-life actively works as a whole unit, strengthening each individual saint to continue the race in the power of the Holy Spirit and to finish strong.

FOR YOUR INFORMATION

"Christ, from whom the whole body, joined and held together by every joint with which it is equipped, when each part is working properly, makes the body grow so that it builds itself up in love" (Ephesians 4:15b–16).

KEEP IN TOUCH—TEXT A FRIEND OR FRIENDS WITH THESE WORDS

There is strength in numbers. Christ would have us, as believers, be unified in our faith for the building up of each other toward maturity in Him. Commit to hang in there together.

TEXT 26
A Different Kind of Normal

JEAN WAS PEEKING IN at her son's playtime. She noticed Brad was just sitting and holding his toys for what seemed like hours. When she called out to him, Brad did not turn his head to look at his mom, as most children would. The second day's response was similar to the first. Unlike most three-year-olds Brad did not play with his toys in a typical manner. When he amused himself with his trains, he did not roll them on the track. Instead, Brad played silently with his trains, holding them up, slowly turning them around and around. By the third day, Jean realized that Brad had not spoken a word for the duration of those days. After months of testing and doctor visits, a report of the findings was at hand. Brad was diagnosed with autism. At first glance, Brad appeared to be like any typical child, but after closer observation, different mannerisms began to show.

Likewise, Christ's disciples first appear to occupy the ordinary concerns of the day, going to work, attending schools and universities, shopping, filling up vehicles at the gas station and the like in a typical manner. Amidst the moments of daily events, some spectators may notice that Christians' reaction in certain incidences appear odd. Filled with the Holy Spirit, we respond with compassion toward those who offend us. We speak words of forgiveness to those who slander us, even when treated badly, we lift them up in prayer. In similar circumstances, onlookers would not consider these behaviors as common place or natural responses. Yet, it is a different description of normal, displayed by those who walk in the way of Christ. As we live and have our being in Him, bystanders observe a spiritual normal that is typical of His followers.

FOR YOUR INFORMATION

"Love your enemies, and do good, and lend, expecting nothing in return, and your reward will be great, and you will be sons of the Most High." (Luke 6:35a).

KEEP IN TOUCH—TEXT A FRIEND OR FRIENDS WITH THESE WORDS

Be caring and loving to those who may spurn you. They will get a chance to see you imitating your heavenly Father, who will find your behavior pleasing in His sight.

TEXT 27
Chocolate Treats (Halloween)

THERE WERE NO DECORATIONS around the house. No fancy pumpkins or smiling skeletons or green-eyed witches on their broomsticks. No spiders hung from trees; no swirly ghosts greeted visitors on the front lawn. Mica thought she would take an opportunity that came around only once a year to share the gospel with children and teens who would come to her door on Halloween. Parents would accompany their little ones in small groups, and teens would follow, dressed as creative characters, with pillow cases to carry the variety of sweet and salty treats they collected.

The moms, dads, teens, and little ones were not aware, however, that earlier that day, Mica had prepared little snack bags with one extra treat no one would expect to find. One by one, Mica placed rich, dark chocolate bites, wrapped with colorful gospel messages, in each snack bag. The message spoke about how sin tricks us, and they told the story of Jesus giving His life for us on the cross—and that became the biggest treat of all because everyone who believed in Him would be pardoned from their sins.

The clock was about to chime six o'clock, and the doorbell would soon begin its continuous ring. A large basket of packaged treats was placed by the door in anticipation of the first guest's arrival. Mica dropped to her knees by the large basket, bowed her head, and softly prayed, asking the Holy Spirit to go before the guests and prepare their hearts to understand the gospel message—that they and their households might be saved. As she lifted her head, Mica heard laughter and parents' voices at her door as she waited for the first ring. The time had come to share the good news.

FOR YOUR INFORMATION

"And the gospel of the kingdom will be proclaimed throughout the whole world as a testimony to all nations ..." (Matthew 24:14).

KEEP IN TOUCH—TEXT A FRIEND OR FRIENDS WITH THESE WORDS

What better time to treat a friend or stranger with the good news of the gospel than during trick-or-treat?

TEXT 28
Hustle and Bustle (Christmas)

It was ten o'clock at night, and Allie frantically was going through lists of toys and presents to order online for family and friends, while looking at the deadline dates to ensure every present would arrive on time for Christmas. Allie kept her pace and finally finished the list around midnight. "Can't wait for Christmas to be over," she admitted to herself, just before falling into a deep sleep.

When her alarm woke her the next morning, she hit the snooze button two times too many. Allie rushed to get dressed and ran out the door, leaving her coffee and bagel behind. After listening to the third Christmas song in her car, she remembered that she needed to order one more gift. "I'll run into one of the department stores during lunch," she said, thinking aloud, "and hopefully I can find something that will work." Allie was trying hard not to be stressed at the start of her day.

Christmas was never meant to be a time of hustle and bustle for anyone. It's a time to slow your pace and celebrate the greatest gift God has given to the world.

And it doesn't come from online shopping or running into department stores among the masses, trying to get that last item on the counter. His gift is not for a day but for a lifetime. "For God so loved the world, that He gave His only Son, that whoever believes in Him should not perish but have eternal life" (John 3:16). The world was condemned because of sin, and Christ came to save the world from that sin through Himself, at no cost to us.

Realizing the true meaning of Christmas, when Christmas Day finally arrived, Allie readied herself to celebrate. The gathering that took place at her home was no longer centered around a Christmas tree and presents. Instead, the family exchanged Christmas stories and laughter and sang carols that retold the story of the baby Jesus and His predicted arrival on earth to save the world from sin. Not only did they recognize Christ's first arrival, but they also considered His second coming, to rule and reign on earth, as Lord of all lords and King of all kings.

FOR YOUR INFORMATION

Remembering the birth of Christ is always a time of celebration for family and friends. We rejoice in what He came to do—to seek and to save lost people from their sins. That thought should free you from the hustle and bustle of the Christmas advent. In its place, focus your thoughts on the redemptive gift that came in the flesh and blood of Jesus Christ.

KEEP IN TOUCH—TEXT A FRIEND OR FRIENDS WITH THESE WORDS

Christmas is not only a time to remember that Jesus came to save the lost but also to remind us to look for His coming back again to rule over all.

TEXT 29
The Close of the Year (New Year's Eve)

THE BRYERS FAMILY PULLED into the last handicapped parking space. Ayers, Ann, and Philip only had to cross the street, walk up the steps, and enter the church building. They were greeted by the warm air relieving them from the extreme cold weather. The clock was chiming its tenth ring as they walked down the aisle, and that's when Ayers decided that the pew midway down was just fine. Meanwhile, across town, families and friends were exchanging stories while waiting to enjoy the end-of-year concert. Others were waiting with friends to be seated at their favorite restaurants, listening for their names to be called, while others were gathered at homes of family and friends, having brought food and drinks, ready to indulge in great company.

The end of the year can be quite daunting when looking back on consequences of poor decisions. The close of the year also can bring a sense of contentment for those who may have relished the success that the year provided. Either way, we don't know what the New Year holds, so as believers, we look to the One who holds the future. God sends the storms and the sunshine in our lives to work His purpose. We only need to be ready to receive them as opportunities to serve Him, in whatever season we experience. On New Year's Eve, the world engages in vast celebrations of the closing of the old and the arriving of the new.

Midnight had arrived. Firecrackers were heard, concerts were at full blast, and restaurants were filled to capacity. Joyous sounds were in the air. In the sanctuary where Ayers, Ann, and Philip were—and in the many other churches—amid a quiet atmosphere of individual prayers carried to the throne of grace, they knelt. For the Bryers, the New Year would be an opportunity to grow and to be strengthened in their faith, remembering that God not only was able to care for them in times of trials but also care for them in the New Year with showers of blessings.

FOR YOUR INFORMATION

Whatever the future brings, be constant in reading the scriptures because "no eye has seen, nor ear heard, nor the heart of man imagined, what God has prepared for those who love Him" (1 Corinthians 2:9).

KEEP IN TOUCH—TEXT A FRIEND OR FRIENDS WITH THESE WORDS

Start the New Year abiding in Christ, and experience the journey as He reveals to you great and mighty things.

TEXT 30
A Song (Good Friday)

GOOD FRIDAY DID NOT sound like a very good Friday for little Judy, who was sitting in a circle, listening to her teacher retell the story that Sunday. "What's so good about Good Friday when Jesus dies?" she asked her dad, who picked her up from class.

"I'll explain it later," Dad responded, while helping her with her sweater. No explanation came, and Good Friday rolled around the following week. Judy was helping her mom rearrange items in the living and dining room. They were expecting family and friends over to celebrate. Lots of food had already been prepared, and others would bring a dish or two as well. Judy found herself getting excited about the preparation for the festivity as she observed the Easter decorations all around her. She walked into her dad's office and noticed a stack of song sheets on the printer. They were copies of songs for the guests to sing later during the gathering.

Picking them up, she began to read some of the lyrics from one hymn titled "At the Cross.":

"Was it for crimes that I have done
He groaned upon the tree?
Amazing pity grace unknown and love
beyond degree.
Well might the sun in darkness hide
And shut His glories in.
When Christ, the mighty Maker, died for
man the creature's sin."

Judy handed the stack of songs to her mom. "What do these verses mean?" she asked as she recalled the story from Sunday's class.

"It means that Christ died on the cross for all of the wrong things we did," Mom began to explain. "Our sins separate us from Him because He is perfectly holy and cannot have sin in His sight. Because God is also perfectly just, He must punish sin, which means He must punish us. Because He loves us so much, God decided to punish His Son, Jesus, instead, to cover all of the wrong we've done. Jesus willingly took our punishment when He died on the cross. So we celebrate every year so we do not forget what Christ did for us."

After hearing that explanation, Judy crouched in the bay window, looking for the first car to approach. She heard the music her mom started playing in the background. It was the same hymn she had read. When Judy saw her dad walking up the driveway, she met him at the door. "I know why Good Friday is good, Dad!" she shouted with glee. "It's because Jesus saved us from punishment for the bad things we've done."

"Yes, that's true," her dad responded, grabbing her in

a big hug. "How did you know that?" "The song told me," she whispered in his ear.

FOR YOUR INFORMATION

"For in Him (Christ) the fullness of God was pleased to dwell, and through Him to reconcile to Himself all things, whether on earth or in heaven, making peace by the blood of His cross" (Colossians 1:19–20).

KEEP IN TOUCH—TEXT A FRIEND OR FRIENDS WITH THESE WORDS

What makes Good Friday good? Jesus's death on the cross, dying for our sins.

TEXT 31

Son Rise (Easter/Resurrection Day)

"IT'S TIME TO WAKE up," whispered Jimmy's dad as eight-year-old Jimmy rubbed his eyes. "If you still want to go with me, you'll have to get up now."

Jimmy jumped out of bed and looked out the window into the dark with excitement. His mom had laid out his clothes the night before so he could wash up and quickly get dressed without her help. He made his way down the stairs to the kitchen, where his dad was already making breakfast. "We're just going to have cereal now, and when we get back home, Mom will have pancakes and bacon waiting for us." That sounded like a plan Jimmy favored. They bowed their heads for grace and then dug into the cereal that crackled with every bite.

His dad went out to start the car and to turn on the defroster while Jimmy finished his cereal and put on his light-blue jacket. "You may want your hat and gloves," his dad suggested since it was a bit cool so early in the morning.

All bundled up, Jimmy and his dad set out into the fading night. "It will be daylight when service is over, right?" the little guy asked, excited about being up so early.

"Yes," his dad said. "It will be daylight."

"Why do they call it sunrise service?" Jimmy asked.

"After Jesus died on the cross for our sins, He was buried, and three days later, very early in the morning, He rose. So we come to worship on Easter morning, which some now call Resurrection Day, to celebrate Jesus's rising from the dead."

Jimmy marveled at those words. He looked out at the sky and saw daylight peeking through the night. He thought, *While the sun rose in the early morning, a long time ago, Jesus, God's Son, was rising too.*

FOR YOUR INFORMATION

"Thus it is written, that Christ should suffer and on the third day rise from the dead, and that repentance and forgiveness of sins should be proclaimed in His name to all nations." (Luke 24:46–47).

KEEP IN TOUCH—TEXT A FRIEND OR FRIENDS WITH THESE WORDS

Every day can be celebrated as Resurrection Day as a reminder that Christ has reconciled you back to God by His death on the cross, and the same power that caused Him to rise from the dead lives in those who believe in Him as their Savior and Lord.

Gotta Text!

YOU HAVE NOW COMPLETED thirty-one days of the gospel message revealed in daily life encounters. Invite your family and friends whom you have been texting to begin their own journeys with their copy of *"Gotta Text!"*, and start a texting network of their own.

"…Comfort one another"…
II Corinthians 11:13b

with God's text messages

About the Author

JULIA A. BROOKS IS a self-described lifelong learner. She completed studies in both the Old and New Testament before proceeding to earn undergraduate and graduate degrees in her chosen disciplines. Presently as an adjunct professor at a Christian university, she engages, encourages and teaches her students how to apply theories and methodologies into the workplace from a biblical perspective. Julia is the founder, CEO and speaker for Paradigm Shift Consulting Group, LLC, an organization that provides professional consultation, support and advocacy for families having individuals with disabilities. As an author, Julia is driven to write devotionals which inspire readers through anecdotes involving everyday life experiences. Julia is married, has two adult children and a grandson.